MW00898755

NATURE *ly*
SPEAKING

"But ask the animals, and they will teach you,

or the birds of the air, and they will tell you;

or speak to the earth, and it will teach you,

or let the fish of the sea inform you."

Job 12:7,8

NATUREly SPEAKING

SPIRITUAL LESSONS FROM OUR NATURAL WORLD

BY DAVID G. HORNBERGER

BERGERPRESS PUBLISHING

2015

Copyright © 2015 by David G. Hornberger

ISBN 978-1-329-77079-9

Second Printing: 2015

BergerPress Publishing

1214 Media Road

Minneola, Florida 34715

http://dehornberger.aimsites.org

Photographs on pages 32, 44, and 62 are by the author. All others
are from iStockphoto and Dollar Photo Club.

NATURE*ly
SPEAKING

This book is dedicated with my love
to my wife Elaine and our four children,
Rachael, Rebecca, Phil, and Andy

CONTENTS

"But ask the animals, and they will teach you, or the birds of the air, and they will tell you; or speak to the earth, and it will teach you, or let the fish of the sea inform you." Job 12:7,8

One day while living in

AFRICA,

I sat under the shade of an ancient Baobab tree watching a herd of elephant bathe, drink, and enjoy the cool water. The rainy season was still weeks away. Except for the tropical lushness around the waterhole, the landscape was a canopy of amber. Dust devils swirled in the distance. Heat waves caused distant herds of wildebeest to shimmer like an out of focus photograph. Except for the chatter of nesting weaverbirds, and an occasional grunt from a grazing animal, the earth was bathed in silence.

Looking through my binoculars the waterhole treated me to an animal paradise. Of course the elephant were the most obvious, but as I watched I started to notice other creatures as well. What looked like a log was actually a crocodile sleeping with its mouth wide open while tickbirds bravely walked in and pecked decayed flesh from between its teeth. Three or four pygmy mongooses chased each other over a pile of rocks. A short distance away, scarab beetles buried orange-sized balls of elephant dung after first laying an egg in its core. Life around the waterhole was a stage of active harmony.

As I watched, I recalled a Bible story about a man who gleaned much of his worldly and spiritual wisdom from God's creation. His name was Job. Usually we remember him because of his sickness and long suffering. But he was also one of the wisest men of his time. He shared his secret of obtaining wisdom in the book bearing his name. In Job 12:7,8 of the New Living Translation he said, "But ask the animals, and they will teach you, or the birds of the air, and they will tell you; or speak to the earth, and it will teach you, or let the fish of the sea inform you."

This led to a lifetime of studying the habits and ways of nature, revealing many spiritual insights that have helped me better understand the ways of God and His plan for mankind. Read on, I gladly share these stories with you to freely use and enjoy!

~ *Dave Hornberger*

NATURE*ly*
SPEAKING

Feather Faith

Have you ever watched a mother hen protect and care for her young? If she sees a hawk circling overhead, she instantly gives a warning sound, and immediately the baby chicks come running to hide beneath her wings.

When menacing storm clouds fill the sky with rolling thunder and jagged lightening, she again makes a noise that beckons her brood to herself where they find protection from the elements.

As night approaches and shadows lengthen, she gives a quiet call that gathers her young to rest.

Under her wings, the chicks are in darkness, not aware of the outside happenings. They trust completely in the sheltering wings to protect them. They are content, safe in their refuge.

NATURE-ly SPEAKING. Dare I parallel God as a "mother hen," and we, His children, as "baby chicks?" If so, there's lots of comfort for us, His chicks, in the Scriptures.

In Luke 13:34 (New Living Translation) Jesus lamented over Jerusalem, "How often I have wanted to gather your children together as a hen protects her chicks beneath her wings, but you wouldn't let me."

Elsewhere, God shows His protection and ample provisions for His own: "He will shield you with His wings. He will shelter you with His feathers. His faithful promises are your armor and protection." (Psalm 91:4,NLT). Again, "I think how much you have helped me; I sing for joy in the shadow of your protecting wings." (Psalm 63: 7, NLT).

Someone once said, "Under His wings many blessings are conferred upon the believer. We are concealed from the enemy, protected from harm, and refreshed by the comforting shade of God's presence when the 'sun' of affliction has beaten upon us."

Many Christians, when going through times of trouble, are encouraged by Psalm 57:1, NLT: "...I look to you for protection. I will hide beneath the shadow of your wings until this violent storm is past."

The Judas Goat

Nature's Hitman

TAKE A GOOD hard look at this picture. You're looking at a killer. "C'mon," you say, "it's only a goat!" You're right it's only a goat. But this is not an ordinary goat. He's a killer by design. When I first laid eyes on this creature, he was already responsible for over 500,000 deaths, and how many more since then, I have no idea. Let me tell you a bit about this particular goat.

First of all, his name is Judas, because he betrays others of his species. He lives in Kenya, East Africa, several miles south-east of Nairobi just off the main Mombasa road. His place of employment is a slaughter-house where tribesmen bring their animals in order to get cash for their material needs. The animals, of course, are slaughtered and sold throughout Kenya to butchers, restaurants, and supermarkets.

I was told Judas was chosen several years ago because he had the stature of a leader. He looked like a goat that other goats and sheep could trust. He was very intelligent and learned his routine very quickly. You see, an East African slaughter-house has holding pens where cattle, sheep, goats, and other livestock are kept. The doomed animals know something is amiss. The smell of blood and death is everywhere. As a result they are very skittish and difficult to lead to the killing rooms. That's where our friend, Judas, comes into the picture. He is taken to a pen housing frightened sheep and goats. His presence is immediately felt. As he mingles with the animals their fears subside and soon they follow him around seeking refuge in the calm, stately, and confident Judas. Once the animals completely trust Judas, a handler opens a gate allowing Judas to go through it along with eight other animals. They faithfully follow him across the compound and he takes them to an elevator door where he patiently waits for the elevator. As the door opens he enters. The others follow. Then he quickly slips out to safety as the iron door slams shut! The others go up to the next floor which is the killing room, and thirty seconds later their throats are slit.

Judas then goes back to the big pen and takes eight more disillusioned followers to the elevator door! All day long he leads sheep and goats to their doom. Of course he doesn't get a paycheck for his grim trade, but he is given his freedom to die a natural death. Actually I saw his predecessor in a nearby pen, happily chewing on a piece of, all things, dried goat meat!

NATURE-ly SPEAKING a spiritual lesson can be learned from the Judas Goat. He is a counterfeit. Other animals that put their trust in him end up dead.

Satan is like the Judas goat. The Devil has laid out an intricate counterfeit plan, so cleverly devised that even Christians must constantly beware lest they fall into his trap.

Satan has counterfeit Christians. Whenever God sows one of His true children, Satan comes along and sows a counterfeit. Jesus explained this in Matthew 13:24-29, 36-43. "(vs.24-29) Here is another story Jesus told: 'The Kingdom of Heaven is like a farmer who planted good seed in his field. But that night as everyone slept his enemy came and planted weeds among the wheat. When the crop began to grow and produce grain, the weeds also grew. The farmer's servants came and told him, Sir the field where you planted that good seed is full of weeds!

'An enemy has done it!' the farmer exclaimed. 'Shall we pull out the weeds?' they asked.

'He replied, 'No, you'll hurt the wheat if you do. Let both grow together until the harvest. Then I will tell the harvesters to sort out the weeds and burn them and to put the wheat in the barn.' "

(vs. 36 – 43) Then, leaving the crowds outside, Jesus went into the house. His disciples said, "Please explain the story of the weeds in the field."

"All right," he said, "I, the Son of Man, am the farmer who plants the good seed. The field is the world, and the good seed represents the people of the Kingdom. The weeds are the people who belong to the evil one. The enemy who planted the weeds among the wheat is the Devil. The harvest is the end of the world, and the harvesters are the angels.

"Just as the weeds are separated out and burned, so it will be at the end of the world. I, the Son of Man, will send my angels, and they will remove from my Kingdom everything that causes sin and all who do evil, and they will throw them into the furnace and burn them. There will be weeping and gnashing of teeth. Then the godly will shine like the sun in their Father's Kingdom. Anyone who is willing to hear should listen and understand."

Satan also has a counterfeit Gospel. In Galations 1:6 it says: "I am amazed that you are turning away so soon from God....you are already following a 'different way [Gospel] to heaven which really doesn't go to heaven at all." (Living Bible)

Satan has counterfeit preachers. Listen: "God never sent those men at all; they are phonies (counterfeits) who have fooled you into thinking they are Christ's apostles." (2 Cor.11:13, L.B.)

Let us learn to know the true Gospel so well that we will not be fooled by the many "counterfeits" of Satan.

NATURE*ly*
SPEAKING

Flight of the Zebra

The zebra is to a lion what a hamburger is to the typical American — a juicy, tasty, meal! But the fact that Mr. King of beasts is often seen eating other, less tasty animals, is proof that the zebra can be a very elusive creature.

Why does the lion fail to kill a zebra 80% (or, 8 in every 10 tries) of the time? Simple.... God has provided the zebra with a very effective escape mechanism. The ability to run away. Fast!

At the slightest inkling of danger, the ever watchful zebra turns hoof and swiftly gallops away, leaving the enemy bewildered, frustrated — and hungry!

NATURE-ly SPEAKING a spiritual lesson can be learned from the flight of the zebra. It's this: when the beast of temptation comes your way, run! Skedaddle! Scram!

Don't try to be a big, brave hero and slug it out eye-ball to eye-ball. You'll fail. Even as a zebra is physically outclassed in an outright fight with a lion, so you will be outclassed in a bout with your spiritual enemy. As cowardly as it might seem, the only safe course is to flee....

The doctrine of "divine flight" is taught throughout scripture. Consider the following examples:

1. Joseph fled from a sexy woman rather than commit adultery. (Gen. 39:15)
2. David fled to god when he felt in danger of "...going along with the unrighteous crowd.." (Ps.143:9)
3. Paul told his Corinth congregation to flee idolatry when he realized they were more interested in the "finer things of life" than the true life of worship. (1 Cor. 10:14)
4. Even preacher Timothy was told to flee youthful lusts. (2 Tim. 2:22)

So, next time your favorite temptation comes along, what are you going to do? That's right...make like a zebra...

Run away.

Fast!

Mongoose Misery

Way back in 1872, a Jamaican sugar planter, W.B. Espeut, was having some serious problems in his fields. Rats! They were all over the place. What to do? Bring in the rat killer brigade, of course! Mongooses. There were none in Jamaica, so he boarded a ship called the "Merchantman," and traveled across the ocean to Calcutta, India. There he captured four male and five female mongooses (one pregnant) and took them back to Jamaica. His solution was so successful he created a new Jamaican export; selling mongooses to sugar cane farmers on other islands.

When word reached the islands of Hawaii, the farmers there saw an answer to their rat problems! So, in 1883, the Hawaiian sugar cane farmers ordered 72 mongooses from the Jamaicans. And, that's when their troubles began....

Oh, yes, the animals got rid of the rats, but their voracious appetites spilled over to feasting on other, ecologically necessary species. An examination of the stomachs of 180 individuals revealed insects, spiders, snails, slugs, frogs, lizards, snakes, birds, eggs of birds and reptiles, all kinds of rodents, crabs, fish and fruits. They also were known to catch mammals many times their size, up to the size of hares and even the young of white-tailed deer. Today Hawaii has more endangered species per square mile than anywhere else on the planet. All this, thanks to the introduction of an innocent rat killer turned monster. It's hard to imagine something so innocent could turn so deadly.

NATURE-ly SPEAKING a spiritual lesson can be learned. Sin often starts very innocently. At the time it might seem very insignificant and, perhaps, useful.

True, the mongoose did a good job getting rid of the rat problem, but that "good" mushroomed into an ecological disaster. Our first parents, Adam and Eve, discovered this sad truth when they ate the forbidden fruit and brought sin into the world. It seemed so innocent and insignificant....

Also, remember Abraham and Lot when they parted company? The story is in Genesis 13. The split was amicable. But what Lot thought was a good move deteriorated into disaster. Read the story and note how gradual was his slide. First he looked, saw, and chose the "fertile plains of the Jordan Valley in the direction of Zoar." (This was his first fatal step.) Next, he moved his tents to a place near Sodom, among the cities of the plain. (That was his second fatal step.) Finally, in Genesis 19 we see him living in sinful Sodom as a respected citizen sitting at the city gate.

Or, remember the story of Samson in Judges chapter 16? His first step downward was falling in love with a Philistiine woman from the enemy camp. Her name was Delilah. This provided the wedge his enemies used to find the secret to his strength. However, before he fell, the crafty prophet outwitted them time after time. But as crafty as he was, the persistence of this determined woman was too much, and he eventually revealed his secret to her which led to his doom.

Both Lot and Samson allowed sin to enter their lives one step at a time. Just like the sugar plantation farmers brought in the mongooses for what seemed like an innocent and sure solution to their problem of rats. But even as the mongooses voracious appetites demanded more and more critters, so sin demands more and more of a person's soul. Even as mongooses brought an ecological disaster to the islands, so sin brings doom, like a cancer, to the soul.

But here's good news! Today, through skilled trappers and certain types of poisons the affected islands are at least fighting back against the mongooses, and in some areas are seeing success.

And here's even greater news! Even though both Lot and Samson were down, they were not doomed. As they cried out to God in repentance, his Grace reached down and restored them. Samson to a feat in his death even greater than all his exploits while living. And Lot was saved with his two daughters from the destruction of Sodom.

In the same way, lives riddled by sin have a sure escape mechanism. No matter where a person is in the cycle of sin, there is redemption through the shed blood of Jesus, the Christ.

The Bible says: "If we confess our sins, he is faithful and just and will forgive us our sins and purify us from all unrighteousness." (1 John 1:9).

When a Nesting Bird Encounters a Storm

There's something peaceful and almost poetic about a nesting bird swaying gently in the arms of a tall sturdy oak. But have you ever watched a nesting bird during a storm? Fierce, angry winds dangerously tipping the nest. Roaring thunder. Lightening slicing the atmosphere. Chaos. Danger. Pelting rain.

What does the feathered creature do? Logically, we would assume a hasty abandonment to safer surroundings. But no...she simply settles as deeply in her nest as possible, fluffs out her feathers, and whichever way the fierce wind shifts she alters her position so as to face directly into it! The bird doesn't flee, but faces the stormy hardship.

NATURE-ly SPEAKING a spiritual principle can be learned from the nesting bird. It's this: In times of stormy hardships, do not run away, but face them head on!

I'm sure you're familiar with the Bible story in Daniel chapter 3 where the three Hebrew captives refused to worship an idol. As a result they were thrown into the "storm" of the firey furnace. They didn't know what the outcome would be, but they willingly faced the storm headon. In this case, the outcome brought honor to God. But sometimes in life the outcome isn't always a happy ending as in this case. Are we willing to face the storm even if the end result is death?

Jesus did that very thing. He faced the storm of "crucifixion." Yet, even this cruel storm did not deter him from his mission. The Bible says in Luke 9:15, "...when the time was come that he (Jesus) should be received up (crucified), he steadfastly set his face to go to Jerusalem (the place of crucifixion, the eye of the storm)." The result of this action assured salvation to all who believe on His name. (Acts 16:31).

The world admires courageous men and women who fearlessly face the storms of life; the Bible demands it!

Listen to
the Mockingbird

The other day while taking one of my walks around the Africa Inland Mission's Retirement Center in Florida, I had a de-ja vu experience. A Mockingbird flew by and perched on a nearby post. The bird fluffed it's feathers, turned around several times as if doing some sort of dance, then as if about to do a virtuoso concert, he straightened his back, perched his tail, arched his head heavenward — and that's when my mind went back some 30 years to an identical scene....a de-ja vu experience!

Inwardly I chuckled, because I knew what was going to happen next. After all, I had seen the same thing 30 years before while taking a similar walk in Pennsylvania. Back then a Mockingbird perched on a similar post, did the feather fluffing bit, even the nervous dance. And, yes, I recalled vividly the straightening of it's back and even the perched tail. And even after all those years I could still remember the breathtaking concert it performed as it "mocked" and wove together songs from a variety of birds.

So, as I fast forwarded to the present, I knew instinctively when this Mockingbird arched his head heavenward, I knew, I just KNEW, I was going to be treated to another thrilling concert! I could hardly wait. After all, I witnessed this before. Right? Wrong!

Oh, yes, the Mockingbird sang all right, but I couldn't believe what my ears were hearing! It's chosen repertoire knocked the prophetic smirk right off my face! Rather than the full-throated oratorios and happy serenades I was expecting, I was treated, instead, to dismal sounds much like the wheezing of an extremely overweight 80 year old on the last lap of a treadmill ma-

"DO NOT BE MISLED: 'BAD COMPANY CORRUPTS GOOD CHARACTER.'" 1 CORINTHIANS 15:33

chine. From this sound the bird morphed into something that sounded like a cross between a hammer and a saw, then it stuttered into something that resembled the mating cry of a distraught crow or some scrub bird. The song concluded much like it began, only the wheezing was more pronounced. I thought, "So much for de-ja vu...."

Puzzled, I went home and did some computer research on Mockingbirds. And there in black and white was my answer. "Mockingbirds," the article said, "imitate not only other birds, but also [sounds] of other animals and even mechanical sounds." It went on to state that the sounds of its environment determines the type of song it sings.

The bird I saw most likely nested and hung out around the workshop on the retirement compound and with the scrub birds and crows that inhabit the area. As a result it's songs reflected the sounds of machines, hammers, saws, toneless birds, and other awful sounds. Whereas my other bird of 30 years past, the de-ja vu bird, lived with songbirds who knew how to carry a tune....

NATURE-ly SPEAKING a spiritual lesson is this: We become like those with whom we associate.

More than likely if we hang out with bad people, we become bad. If we hang out with good people, there's an excellent chance we'll gravitate to good things. Did you ever notice how married couples often use the same expressions, intonations, and, some say, even start to look alike?

Scripture makes some very interesting statements about this topic. In 1 Corinthians 15:33 (NIV) it says, "Do not be misled: 'Bad company corrupts good character.' "

In the same book, 1 Corinthians 5:9-11 (NIV), Paul explains that the "bad company" are not the unsaved, but those who say they are Christians! He says, "I have written you in my letter not to associate with sexually immoral people — not at all meaning the people of this world who are immoral, or to the greedy or swindlers, or idolaters. In that case you would have to leave this world. But now I am writing you that you must not associate with anyone who calls himself a brother but is sexually immoral or greedy, an idolater or a slanderer, a drunkard or a swindler. With such a man do not even eat." Wow!

As missionaries, pastors, true believers, our task of discipling new believers requires holy discernment. Clearly we must be patient with those who are growing in the faith, and continue in fellowship with them in spite of the sin they often stumble into, or are yet unaware of. But when a professing Christian willfully rejects the light, or is consistently disobedient, we are commanded to discern this and break fellowship.

The reason for this discrimination is brought out clearly in 2 Timothy 3:1-5 (Philips translation): "But you must realize that in the last days the times will be full of danger. Men will become utterly self-centered, greedy for money, full of big words. They will be proud and abusive, without any regard for what their parents taught them. They will be utterly lacking in gratitude, reverence and normal human affections. They will be treacherous, reckless and arrogant, loving what gives them pleasure instead of loving God. They will maintain a facade of 'religion,' but their life denies its truth. Keep clear of people like that."

However, before writing anyone off, please heed the admonition of Galatians 6:1-2 (Philips Translation): "Even if a man should be detected in some sin, my brothers, the spiritual ones among you should quietly set him back on the right path, not with any feeling of superiority but being yourselves on guard against temptation. Carry each other's burdens and so live out the law of Christ. Let us not be weary in doing good, for at the proper time we will reap a harvest if we do not give up."

How to be a Jackass for Jesus

The Donkey, sometimes referred to as a Jackass, has played a rather obscure part in history, being out-shown by his flashy cousin, the horse. However, for many poor communities it has been an excellent servant, useful both as a work animal and for riding. It requires little upkeep — mainly, food and warmth.

It's difficult to establish how the donkey was domesticated. Wall and cave paintings show that it entered history at a very early date. The earliest

Egyptian dynasties, around 4000 B.C., bred donkeys. The Romans made use of the donkey as a beast of burden in their military expeditions. As a general rule, wild donkeys live in dry, if not desert, regions. They have been driven to do so because all the better areas have been taken by man for use as pasture. Needing little food, they have adapted very well to the harsh conditions of their habitat. The donkey is courageous, hard-working and recovers quickly from fatigue. Often ill-fed and ill-treated, it nevertheless does its work with determination.

NATURE-ly SPEAKING, a spiritual principle can be gleaned from the donkey. In teaching the topic of "humility" and "servanthood" to His disciples, Christ chose a time when each one was trying to find out who would be sitting in the seat of authority in the new Kingdom. Said Jesus, "You know that in this world kings are tyrants, and officials lord it over the people beneath them. But among you it should be quite different. Whoever wants to be a leader among you must be your servant, and whoever wants to be first must become your slave. For even I, the Son of Man, came here not to be served but to serve others, and to give my life as a ransom for many." (Matthew 20:25-28, New Living Bible.) In other words, Jesus wanted (and still wants) His followers to be like the donkey — a humble servant.

It was this very spirit of service that prompted Jesus to wash the feet of the disciples, showing them the ultimate in humility.

As Christians we are to be cheerful servants, clothed in humility. Special "how to be a humble servant" instructions are laid out in Ephesians 6:5-8. It says humble servants should:

- ... obey their masters. In today's language this simply means to be faithful employees. (If you are an employer, read verse 9.)
- ... should be conscientious in service. Verse five points out that "servants" are to work with a singleness of heart. In other words, full dedication.
- ... should not serve simply so things "look good." (vs.6)
- ... should do the Will of God from the heart. (vs.6)
- ... should render cheerful service to men as you would to the Lord.
- ... finally, a Christian servant should realize that even if he is not properly paid by man, he will be by God. (vs.8)

Godliness is humility.

Camouflage: Now You See'um, Now You Don't

Camouflage is a handy gift God has given to the critters of the wild. Camouflage helps protect against predators; at the same time, it helps predators sneak up on its target without being seen.

Camouflage is defined as "...concealment through absence of contrast." This lack of contrast between an animal and its background is due to certain physical qualities such as the over-all texture and color of the body covering. Every time you walk through the fields or woods you may pass right by a creature and never see it. Because of its lack of contrast, it blends in deceptively with weeds, foliage or trees.

When you look at an object, you clearly see its colors and varying tones. But the thing your eye is mainly taken with is its silhouette. In camouflage, the silhouette is broken up. Look at the pictures above. The first is a frog, and he's pretty well concealed without much of a silhouette showing. The next is a bird almost the same color and markings as the tree bark. While the silhouette of the butterfly is pronounced, still, its design resembles a flower bud. The roaring lion, on the other hand, is downright frightening. Anyone seeing it — in full silhouette — would either be frozen with fear, or would turn and run away as fast as possible.

NATURE-ly SPEAKING several spiritual lessons can be learned from camouflage.

The Bible says that Satan is like a roaring lion. I'm sure most sane people would not be inclined to cozy up to it. Quite the opposite. They'd break Olympic records dashing away. Of course, the wily devil is aware of his fearful reputation, so, like the deceiver that he is, he resorts to disguise and camouflage to trap his victims. Often he transforms himself into "...an angel of light...." causing people to believe he is good when in reality he is worse than bad, he's evil! I'm sure this is the background of today's cults, isms, and false religions.

Unfortunately many Christians look at a "camouflaged" gospel. To them it is not in sharp silhouette. They don't see or understand it's message, therefore, they cannot apply its principles to their lives. They just don't get it! An interesting story is told in Mark 8:14-18: Jesus had just miraculously fed one group of 5000 men and later, 4000 people. Then, he and his disciples left the area, got into a boat and started crossing the lake. The Bible says, (vs 14-18) "But the disciples discovered they had forgotten to bring any food, so there was only one loaf of bread with them in the boat. As they were crossing the lake, Jesus warned them, "Beware of the yeast of the Pharisees and of Herod." They decided he was saying this because they hadn't brought any bread. Jesus knew what they were thinking, so he said, "Why are you so worried about having no food? Won't you ever learn or understand? Are your hearts too hard to take it in? You have eyes — can't you see? You have ears — can't you hear? Don't you remember anything at all? What about the 5000 men I fed with five loaves of bread?...." Somehow the disciples, even though they saw, heard, and even participated in the miracles Jesus had just performed did not apply the truth to themselves. They were still looking at a "camouflaged" gospel. To them it was not in sharp silhouette. As a result, they, like many of us, could not live by its principles.

Let us faithfully study God's Word, the Bible, asking God for wisdom so we can understand it in sharp contrast and blazing silhouette.

The Snake Killer

T he Secretary Bird, standing four feet tall and with a fierce hawk-like head, owes its existence to the creepy world of snakes. Methodically criss-crossing the vast African plains, it approaches a venomous snake with caution, using its wings to ward off the snake's attempt to bite. One swift peck breaks the snake's neck. The bird then eats the body, but not the head.

A strong flyer, the Secretary Bird nevertheless prefers to walk or run on the ground. But this preference brings a certain woe to this feathered snake-hunter. Often, immediately after a kill, other birds swoop down in an attempt to steal the snake. On such occasions, the Secretary Bird, rather than easily flying away from the predator tries to run away. Invariably he looses his dinner!

NATURE-ly SPEAKING a spiritual lesson can be learned from the Secretary Bird's preference to run rather than fly.

The Christian also has wings — wings of prayer. At any time he can mount up upon those wings. But often he doesn't use them. He'd rather run. Rather than, "taking his problems to the Lord in prayer" he often tries to figure out a solution on his own. As a result, his troubles swiftly overcome. In the Old Testament of the Bible, King Jehoshaphat was surrounded by his enemy. He frantically looked for a way of escape. There was none. Doomed! But then he remembered he had the "wings of prayer." So he used them by crying to God in prayer. The Bible tells us what happened as a result. II Chronicles 18:31 says, "...the Lord helped him; and God moved them (his enemies) to depart from him." Simple!

Jesus said, "But if you stay in Me and obey My commands, you may ask any request you like, and it will be granted! (John 15:7, Living Bible.)

Quit running; instead, use your "wings of prayer."

All Puffed Up
and Nowhere to Go

Many, many moons ago, at least 30 or 40 years, while living in Kenya, a group of us "up country" missionaries jammed our families in cars and headed for a vacation to coastal Momba- sa. Rather than dodging potholes over macadam roads as in modern times, we rattled along on dirt and "washboard" ones with periodic stops to fix flat-tires.

Once we arrived and were unpacked, everyone could hardly wait to splash into the Indian ocean to collect shells, and observe the coral reefs.

One day, I think it was Shel Arensen, caught one of the strangest crea- tures I ever saw! It was a Porcupine fish, a spiky member of the Puffer fish family. The reason Shel was able to pluck the fish from the ocean is because "puffers" are weak swimmers and often just bob along on currents. Also, they are among the few fish that feed on coral, undeterred by its hard lime- stone. They just nip off its branches and then crush the coral to a gritty pulp before swallowing. They also eat mollusks like oysters and clams, crunching the hard shells with ease.

But the really unique thing about the Porcupine fish is its defense system. Swimming along with its spines relaxed, it may look like an easy prey to a large marine predator. But looks can be deceptive. When attacked the Porcupine fish gulps down water and puffs itself up into a floating sphere covered by fearsome spines, some up to two inches long. Smart predators make a hasty exit. Those that don't end up very dead. Even formidable hunters such as sharks and barracudas have been found dead with puffed-up Porcupine fish stuck in their throats.

NATURE-ly SPEAKING a spiritual application can be gleaned from the process of becoming "puffed-up." As we have just read, Porcupine fish puff themselves up as a defensive manoeuver. Birds, on the other hand, "puff-up" their feathers to keep warm. However, in the human realm, when someone is "puffed-up" the term often refers negatively to someone who has an excessively high opinion of himself.

The Bible refers to people who are "puffed-up" as proud, arrogant, conceited. The proud person looks at himself differently than God looks at him. Pride is a "mental attitude sin" and is listed in Proverbs 6:16-19 as one of the seven worst sins.

Unfortunately the sin of being "puffed up" is alive and well in Christian circles. Often we become "puffed-up experts" in passing judgement on a ministry or decision without giving any constructive input.

We become critical, or cynical when, if only we gave our support and encouragement, our input might very well have spelled the success for a particular project, program, or person. I think, perhaps, Paul's statement in 1 Corinthians 8:1, could very well apply in this instance. It says, "[Superficial] knowledge puffs up, but love builds up."

And what is love? "Love is patient and kind. Love is not jealous or boastful or proud or rude. Love does not demand its own way. Love is not irritable, and it keeps no record of when it has been wronged. It is never glad about injustice but rejoices whenever the truth wins out. Love never gives up, never loses faith, is always hopeful, and endures through every circumstance. (1 Corinthians 13:4-7, New Living Translation.)

NATURE*ly*
SPEAKING

V is for Victory

Have you every wondered why geese fly in the "V" formation? For years, specialists in aerodynamics wondered the same thing. Two engineers calibrated in a wind tunnel what happens in a "V" formation. Each goose, in flapping his wings, creates an upward lift for the bird that follows. When all the birds do their part in the "V" formation, the entire flock has a 71% greater flying range than if each bird flew alone.

Each depends on the other to get to it's destination. Every bird in the formation takes a turn at being the lead bird. The strong birds encourage the weak with their incessant honking.

Also, if a goose becomes ill or exhausted, a stronger bird drops out of flight with it, and, together, they find a resting place. The strong one stands patiently by, guarding, until the weak one once again gains strength to fly.

For these large birds "V," indeed, is for "victory."

NATURE-ly SPEAKING some spiritual observations can be gleaned from this flight pattern. By flying in this formation, each bird assists each other in reaching the goal. Christianity isn't competition. Our goal should be one that helps the entire "body" reach it's ultimate goal. With a loving and non-judgmental attitude, each of us should reach out to the idle, the weak, the strong, and practice patience with the fallen. The birds do it, so should Christians.

I love the way the Apostle Paul talks to the church in 1 Thessalonians 5: 14, 15, "Brothers and sisters, we urge you to warn those who are lazy. Encourage those who are timid. Take tender care of those who are weak. Be patient with everyone. See that no one pays back evil for evil, but always try to do good to each other and to everyone else."

Along with the above verses, take time to read Galatians 6:1-10 and try to weave these truths into your daily walk with God as well. The birds accomplish their victory by lovingly working together in harmonious fellowship. I'm sure if Christians put this type of activity into practice, the world would sense a spiritual stirring rivaled only by Pentecost itself!

The Survival Kit
of the Desert

The camel is designed for desert living. It's eyes are protected against sand and sun by three sets of lids. It's feet are broad and padded, ideal for walking on hot sand. One big drink of water will last for days.

To desert people, the camel is a "burden-bearer." An adult carries loads averaging 500 pounds.

When fierce sandstorms blow, the kneeling camel becomes a "shelter" for it's master.

If the traveler gets lost, the humped creature becomes a "guide" by leading him to a life-saving oasis of water.

Desert people drink camel milk, eat camel meat, build fires with dried camel dung, use camel skin to make their tents, and carve utensils from camel bones.

Indeed, the camel is the survival-kit of the desert — without this beast desert people would most likely die.

NATURE-ly SPEAKING some spiritual lessons can be learned from the camel. For instance:

Even as the camel is designed for desert living, so Jesus Christ was specially "designed" to come to this world as a sacrifice for sin. As a result, "...whosoever believes on Him, shall not perish but have everlasting life. (John 3:16).

Likewise, Jesus Christ is a "burden-bearer." Isaiah 53:4 says, "Surely he hath borne our griefs, and carried our sorrows...."

He is a "shelter," as prophetically proclaimed in Psalm 61:3, "For thou hast been a shelter for me, and a strong tower from the enemy."

Most important, Jesus is a "guide." The Bible says He came "...to give light to them that sit in darkness and in the shadow of death, to guide our feet into the way of peace. (Luke 1:79)."

Why not let Jesus Christ be your "burden-beared," "shelter," and "guide" by personally committing your life to Him?

The Curse
of the Baobab

I n Africa there is a weird-looking tree known as the Baobab. Strange tales of superstition surround it. With stubby trunk and root-like branches, African tribesmen solemnly claim it is cursed. They say the Baobab at one time was the most beautiful of all trees; but because of it's beauty, it became proud. Result? God pulled it up by the roots and shoved it back down into the earth, upside down!

The close association with the legendary downfall of this tree and the Biblical account of Satan's fall – through pride – causes superstitious terror among some African tribes. They claim the Baobab is the home of the earth's evil spirits. It is not unusual for non-Christians to offer sacrifices under the tree to appease the evil spirits.

NATURE-ly SPEAKING, this legend can teach us something about God. He hates pride; but loves humility. The writer of Proverbs puts it this way, "A man's pride shall bring him low; but honor shall uphold the humble in spirit." (Proverbs 29:23)

Listen to the humble words of tall, handsome, Saul, Israel's first king-elect, "Am not I a Benjamite, of the smallest of the tribes of Israel? and my family the least of all the families of the tribe?" (1 Samuel 9:21). But later in life this same humble hero becomes a sniveling, suspicious, suicide case. Why? With responsibility, fame, riches, and power came pride. That five letter word finished him off.

Now listen to the humble words of the slingshot ace, David, Israel's second king-elect, "Who am I, O Lord God? And what is my house, that thou hast brought me hitherto? (2 Samuel 7:18)

Later in life God called this hero a "man after His own heart." Why this honor to one king and not the other? Despite responsibility, fame, riches, and power, David retained his humility. These eight letters spell his glory.

The difference between Saul and David was the difference between pride and humility. Somewhere between these two men stand you and me.

Where?

NATURE*ly SPEAKING

The Case of the Flabby Cod

Sea food lovers enjoy cod. But the process from ocean to frying pan is rather interesting…. Cod fishermen bring their catch "live" to the marketplace by keeping them in holding tanks aboard their ships. However, a serious problem arose when they realized the cod flesh became soft and flabby by the time they got to the market. The problem was isolated to the fact that the fish, after they were caught and placed in the holding tank, just lay in the bottom and didn't move. Thus the flesh became soft and flabby.

But the crafty fishermen soon discovered an ingenious way to keep the cod swimming and strong while in the holding tanks. They simply put several large catfish in the tank with the cod. These two species of fish are natural enemies. The very presence of a catfish in the same tank caused the cod to swim around to stay away from any stings and jabs. As a result the cod remained active and healthy, not flabby. Worthy of marketplace scrutiny.

NATURE-ly SPEAKING a spiritual lesson can be learned from this process.

Sometimes Christians mirror the cod fish in the tank. We live in our own little world and are content to take it easy and do as little as possible. We're surrounded by our own kind. We accept the status quo. As time goes by we become spiritually soft and flabby.

I'm sure God sometimes allows a "catfish" into our lives in order to keep us active, provoked, and strong spiritually. The "catfish" may be a wayward offspring, a fellow employee or employer, a classmate, a fellow church member, maybe even the pastor! You know, those people who "get under your skin." Those people who are a constant irritation. They try our very patience and self-control. But, you know, as we deal with these people we're forced to seek solutions, often through prayer and searching the Bible. And even through concerned confrontation. As a result, we start developing spiritual muscle we never had before.

In James 1:2-4 of the New Living Translation, the author put it all in perspective, "Dear brothers and sisters, whenever trouble comes your way, let it be an opportunity for joy. For when your faith is tested, your endurance has a chance to grow. So let it grow, for when your endurance is fully developed, you will be strong in character and ready for anything."

NATURE*ly* SPEAKING

Nature's Choo Choo Train

Someone has wisely said, "It is a form of insanity to do the same things over and over and then expect different results."

Case in point: the processionary caterpillar. The noted French naturalist, Jean Henri Fabre', studied this unique caterpillar in great detail. What makes it so unique is its instinct to follow, in lock step, the one in front. This behavior not only gives the caterpillar its name, but also a deadly characteristic.

Fabre' took a flowerpot and placed a number of caterpillars in single-file around the circumference of the pot's rim. Each caterpillar's head touched the one in front of it. Next he placed their favorite food in the middle of the circle within easy sight and reach. As the procession began each caterpillar followed the one in front thinking it was headed for the food. Round and round they went, for seven days! After a week of this mindless activity, the critters started to drop dead due to exhaustion and starvation. All they had to do to avoid death was to stop the routine of senseless circling, break rank, and head directly to the food, less than six inches away.

But in their procession around the pot, they were blindly following their instincts, routine, habits, past experiences, tradition, custom and precedent — the way they had always done things. The result? Death.

NATURE-ly SPEAKING we can glean several spiritual lessons from this caterpillar's behavior. But the one I want to focus on is the killer known as, routine. People, churches, organizations, and even governments get caught up in this death trap.

If you're a guy, raise a beard.
If you have one, shave it off.

D id you ever see a living dead man? Maybe, if you carefully look into a mirror you might see one! You know, rise at 6 a.m., brush teeth at 6:05, shower at 6:10, breakfast at 6:30, say "good morning" to spouse at 6:35, leave for work at 6:57, work from 8 to 5 with noontime lunch break to eat peanut butter and apricot jam sandwich, arrive home at 5:20, say "hello" to spouse at 5:25, eat dinner at 5:30 p.m., watch news at 6 p.m., have family time from 7 to 9 by watching game shows on TV, have devotions at 9:15, go to bed at 10 p.m. You know, the old "processionary caterpillar" death rattle.

Be brave! Throw away the palate of greys and dull browns. Use a broad brush and blend some red, yellow, green, blue, over life's canvas. The masterpiece will be a new you!

Forget devotions at 9:15 p.m. — try them at 5 a.m. or during lunch break. And for-goodness-sake replace the jam and peanut butter sandwich with something, like, maybe...an Indian curry dish on Monday, then a Chinese scorpion on Tuesday, etc.

And while you are making changes try new ways to get to work. Walk, ride bicycle, car pool, buy a motorcycle. Take different routes. Listen to your spouse tell about their day. Ask questions. Laugh together. Eat out from time to time. If you're a guy, raise a beard. If you have one, shave it off. If you're a gal, don't raise a beard. If you have one, shave it off. Quick! Get on your computer and read quotes by Yogi Berra or Muhammad Ali. Maybe once a month forget to brush your teeth — chew gum instead! In other words, D-I-V-E-R-S-I-F-Y.

Study the life of Jesus. He knew the value of diversity. When He wasn't climbing hills or trudging through towns, he was walking on water. He

If you're a gal, don't raise a beard.
If you have one, shave it off. Quick!

preached to congregations in synagogues and bars, on street corners, even to a congregation of one in a Sycamore tree. He enjoyed partying with the rich and privileged as well as the poor and downtrodden. He loved kids. He told stories. He wept. One time He prayed so hard that blood came from His pores! Each day for Jesus, was different. He raged at people who defiled the temple. He calmed the sea when His disciples were in peril. He lived, he died, he rose. A life of routine? Never!

Let's never get lost in the quagmire of routine like the processionary caterpillar. But let us be bold and use our talents and gifts in such a way that our life will always be fresh and relevant.

The Cliff Dweller

The African Klipspringer when full grown, stands only about two feet tall. Yet the animal is amazing in design. His small horns act like duel daggers in close combat. His large ears, keen sense of smell, and sharp eyes are instant warning systems of danger. Perhaps the most remarkable aspect about the Klipspringer is his ability to defy gravity. A cliff dweller, this little creature darts from rock to rock with nimbleness almost unbelievable. To the Klipspringer it matters not if the path be horizontal or perpendicular, up or down, he fearlessly streaks over any treacherous terrain. The reason he can do this is because of his hoof's design. Upon close examination the animal looks as if he is running on tiptoe. Actually, God designed his hoof to act like a suction cup. The design keeps the Klipspringer from slipping.

NATURE-ly SPEAKING a spiritual principle can be learned from the Klipspringer's hoof. Even as God has given this animal a device to keep it from slipping, likewise He does the same for the Christian.

The Bible says in 2 Samuel 22:37, "Thou hast enlarged my steps under me; so that my feet did not slip...." He does this in various ways. One, He has given us a conscience which determines within us when we do right or wrong. But sometimes the conscience can become seared...useless.

So as a back-up protection, God has given Angels. Psalm 91:11 says, "For He shall give His angels charge over thee, to keep thee in all thy ways."

In addition, Christians have the Holy Spirit indwelling as an additional safety factor. Add to this the bountiful protective devices provided throughout Scripture by God the Father and the Son!

With all these protective devices, we need not fear the world and its evils. We can live for Christ each day with no fear of slipping. "Wherefore, seeing we also are compassed about with so great a cloud of witnesses, let us lay aside every weight, and the sin which doth so easily beset us, and let us run with patience the race that is set before us." (Hebrews 12:1).

Dung for Dinner

I magine! Dung for dinner! That's right, animal droppings. What's more the Scarab Beetle loves and thrives on the stuff. The critter will even kill in his quest for dung. This beetle lives on the hot, barren desert and semi-desert areas of North and East Africa where it lives on dung. When it senses a fresh pile of dung nearby, the scarab hurries toward it. Using its sharp-edged head and forelegs much like a manure-spreader, the beetle pushes pieces of dung under its belly. Then with it's four back legs it tosses and shapes them into a ball which sometimes gets as large as an orange.

The beetle makes and buries two kinds of dungballs. One is a food ball. The other is a ball in which the female beetle lays an egg. When the egg hatches inside the ball, the larva eats the dung. After one to three months the pupa has become an adult, and the new beetle crawls out.

When making a dungball, the beetle has to work fast lest other scarabs steal it. If such an attempt is made a terrible fight takes place. Sometimes several beetles get killed in the battle. We laugh and say, "Wow! All that fuss over a little bit of dung! C'mon, get real!!"

NATURE-ly SPEAKING a spiritual parallel can be drawn by the way some christians behave. All too often our lives mirror the Scarab Beetle. We fuss, fume, storm-around, make-a-lot-of-noise over insignificant things which amount to no more than a "bit of dung" in God's overall plan. Sometimes we get so busy throwing dung we forget the greatest command of all, "Love your neighbor as yourself."

How many church splits, broken relationships, and yes, even deaths (I personally know of two) have resulted from small insignificant disagreements or viewpoints which, in God's sight are no more than "a bit of dung."

I dare say, dung is a great fertilizer. I humbly suggest whenever spiritual dung comes our way, we use it as fertilizer by plowing it into some fertile soil, and grow love and understanding for those around us.

Prof. Glasser wrote, "There is no mental illness, just people who need to love and be loved." A loving attitude is a sign of spiritual maturity. Ephesians 4:15 says, "But speaking the truth in love, may grow up into him in all things, which is the head, even Christ."

"And the Lord make you to increase and abound in love one toward another, and toward all men...." (1 Thess. 3:12).

Happiness is a Two-way Street

Elephants are like humans in many ways. They spank their babies, express joy and sorrow, nurse their sick, clown around, fight, and, at times practice birth-control.

Once, while photographing in an African swamp, I saw a downcast elephant whom I immediately nick-named, Sadsack. He just stood munching slowly on swamp grass. His drooping eyes matched his drooping ears. Sadsack didn't even stir when another Proboscidian slushed his bulk to within a foot of those dejected eyes. But Mr. drop-in-for-awhile knew exactly how to handle old Sadsack. First, he gave his blue buddy a tender trunk rub. Then, he raised his trunk and trumpeted a hearty, back-slapping greeting. Then, showing the ultimate in elephant friendship, gave old Sadsack a mighty trunk-hug!

Suddenly Sadsack wasn't sad anymore. A twinkle seemed to gleam in his eyes. He stood straighter. The two friends rubbed heads, gave trunk-hugs again, and eventually had a delightful feast of swamp grass together.

You see, a sad elephant was made happy by a friendly gesture; and as a result, I'm sure the one who offered the friendly gesture was made even happier. You see, happiness is a two-way street.

NATURE-ly SPEAKING a spiritual principle can be gleaned. If we sow friendship and happiness we reap friendship and happiness.

I'm convinced much of today's unhappiness and depression is simply because, in this "me first" generation, people have lost the fine art of making others happy.

Try an experiment. For one month, try to make someone happy every day, either by kind words or kind deeds. I'm sure, at the end, you'll discover a new, happier, and more positive, you!

God presents this principle in Proverbs 27:17, "As iron sharpens iron, a friend sharpens a friend."

Try it!

Happiness is a two-way street!

NATURE*ly* SPEAKING

The Okapi's Hiding Place

The Uturi Rainforest in Africa's Congo provides the perfect hiding place for a very shy animal known as the Okapi. It looks like a combination between a mule, a zebra, and a giraffe. The forest people known as Pygmies were the first to discover it. They told the outside world that there was a very strange looking animal roaming deep within the jungle. They described it as best they could and even tried to draw pictures showing its strange features.

Naturalists were interested, but after months of futile efforts to find the animal gave up the hunt assuming the Pygmies were "seeing things."

However, in the 1940's the Pygmy hunters were able to get close enough to one of the shy animals to shoot it with bow and arrow. They immediately skinned it and took the skin to a Naturalist. The proof was in!

Since that time others have been found and some have even been brought out of Africa to live in zoos. The animal is an ancestor to the giraffe. Some Scientists claim this is the animal that Noah brought into the ark and which eventually, over hundreds of years, developed into the long-necked giraffe of today.

But the amazing thing about the Okapi is that it was able to stay hidden for such a long time. It probally lived in the Uturi Rainforest ever since it got out of the Ark and wasn't discovered until 5000 years later.

NATURE-ly SPEAKING a spiritual lesson can be observed from the Okapi. Even though it was able to hide its existence for 5000 years, it was eventually discovered. This also applies to our lives and our sins. Often we can keep sins hidden from man, but never from God. Even as He knew the Okapi existed, so He knows when we sin.

Take King David as an example. In his case when he sinned with another man's wife, God knew. But eventually the entire sordid mess came out in the open. (Read the entire story starting with 2 Samuel 12.) God told David in verse 12, "You did it secretly, but I will do this to you openly in the sight of all Israel."

But on a brighter note, as God saw fit to hide the Okapi for at least 5000 years in the deep jungles of Africa, likewise He often hides Christians from their enemies. We can comfort ourselves as we read Psalms 27:5 where God gives us a promise, "For in the time of trouble he shall hide me in his pavilion; in the secret of his tabernacle shall He hide me...."

Psalms 119:114 — "Thou art my hiding place."

(Dear reader: While doing research, I discovered the Uturi forest pygmies also claim there are other strange animals roaming in unexplored areas of this vast rainforest. They say there is an animal that even breathes fire. And when shown pictures of many different types of creatures, they consistently point to the dinosaur types as the one they saw. Who knows? Could it be there is still some type of dinosaur roaming unexplored corners of this world?)

NATURE *ly* SPEAKING

The Caterpillar that got a Haircut

I n the booklet, Illustrations From Nature, Virginia Whitman tells of a caterpiller that got a fatal haircut by a hoard of ants. It was covered with close-growing bristles that appeared to protect its tender body from the onslaught of the hungry ants. At first the ants were unable to penetrate the hairy armor. They could not get between the bristles nor could they reach the caterpillar on his underside where there were not bristles. Those that tried could easily be fended off. Finally the ants settled on a new strategy. They began biting off short bits of bristle all over its body. With determined steadfastness the ants barbered away at the caterpillar until they were able to reach past the stubble and bite into the tender skin. Before long the ants had made a complete conquest of the caterpillar and were able to cut him up into ant-sized chunks that could be carried off to their nest.

NATURE-ly SPEAKING this incident presents us with a Scriptural principal. It's possible that our strongest point may become our point of vulnerability.

Remember Samson and his haircut? (If not read, Judges 16:4-22). Briefly, Samson had extraordinary strength and was dedicated a Nazirite from birth to death. He was brash. Overconfident, fearing no one. He was also one of God's judges, and his enormous strength lay in these words he confessed to his worldly, not-so-nice, double-crossing, girlfiend, Delilah, "My hair has never been cut, for I was dedicated to God as a Nazirite from birth. If my head were shaved, my strength would leave me, and I would become as weak as anyone else." This was all the sly Delilah needed to know. So when he fell asleep she clipped off his hair, then turned him over to the Philistine leaders for nice profit. They in turn gouged out his eyes and put him in prison.

Like Samson, it's possible for us to assume that we are above attack by Satan, or impervious to his devices. And in this state of mistaken self-confidence, we, like the caterpillar and Samson, meet our downfall.

"If you think you are standing strong, be careful, for you, too, may fall into the same sin." (1 Corinthians 10:12, New Living Translation.)

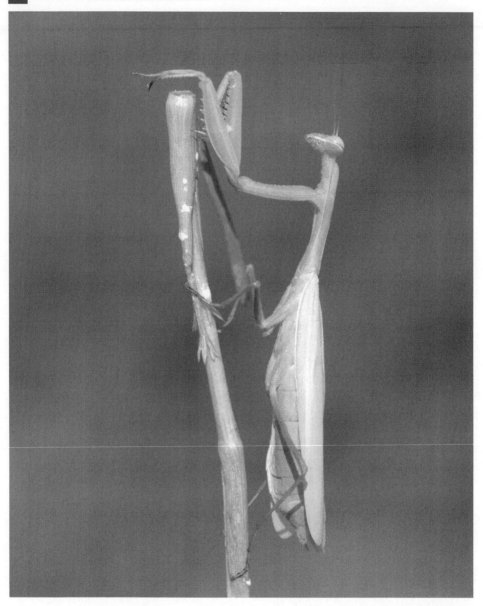

NATURE*ly*
SPEAKING

The Pious Cannibal

The Praying-mantis has been called the "dinosaur" of the insect world because of it's almost prehistoric-looking body. Unlike other insects, the mantis has the ability not only to move it's head in such a way as to look over it's shoulder, it can wash it's face cat-fashion. It can even lower it's head and drink like a horse! And if you ever catch one for a pet, you'll soon discover it will take food from your hand.

Even though the mantis gives the appearance of being in an attitude of prayer, it can be very nasty. As a female mantis matures, and particularly when she is carrying eggs, her one consuming desire is to eat. In her quest for food she devours other members of the mantis family, including her own mate.

Can you believe this?....even when the male is in the mating process of fertilizing hundreds of the female's eggs she turns on him. She'll clutch him in her saw-toothed forelegs, turn her arrow-shaped head backwards, bite off his head and placidly start chewing down his thorax. As soon as the fertilization is completed she eats all of him!

NATURE-ly SPEAKING, a spiritual principle can be learned from the cannibalistic nature of this pious looking insect.

> The mantis reminds me of some pharisaical (or, sometimes referred to as "holier-than-thou") types. Outwardly they take on an attitude of prayerful spirituality; inwardly, however, they are ready to pounce, rip-apart, and devour others.

The mantis reminds me of some pharisaical (or, sometimes referred to as "holier-than-thou") types. Outwardly they take on an attitude of prayerful spirituality; inwardly, however, they are ready to pounce, rip-apart, and devour others. They are the cause of constant turmoil, especially within the framework of a church body.

The Apostle Paul describes this type of person as one who is controlled by "his own sinful desires." He says in 1 Corinthians 3:1-3, "Dear Brothers and Sisters, when I was with you I couldn't talk to you as I would to mature Christians. I had to talk to you as though you belonged to this world or as though you were infants in the Christian life. I had to feed you with milk and not with solid food, because you couldn't handle anything stronger. And you still aren't ready, for you are still controlled by your own sinful desires. You are jealous of one another and quarrel with each other. Doesn't that prove you are controlled by your own sinful desires?"

I believe these "mantis Christians" are used by Satan to cause the unsaved to ignore the Christian faith. God warns these people in the strongest of terms when He said in Luke 17:2, "It were better for him that a millstone were hanged about his neck, and be cast into the sea."

Unfortunately, "mantis Christians" can be found in most every type of Christian organization. They not only make everyone around them miserable, but they feel miserable themselves. (I'm not sure, but maybe it's a "stage" we all go through. I'd appreciate any comments and insight you

might have.) Someone has said, "Every saint (Christian) has a past, and every sinner has a future."

But, of this I am convinced, God's love and forgiveness can take every "mantis Christian" and change them to be a positive force within the body of Christ. (So, never, never give up on them.) All that's needed is a healthy and humble application of the same Biblical formula that any Christian who sins uses to get back into a mature fellowship with God. It's simply following the instruction found in 1 John 1:9 which says, "If we confess our sins to Him, He is faithful and just to forgive us and to cleanse us from every wrong."

After that, it's a joyful step into a dynamic Christian life filled with peace, joy, and fellowship with fellow believers.

Nature's Missionary:
The Red-billed Oxpecker

The grazing animals of Africa's grasslands are blessed by a bird that not only acts as a warning system, but keeps them healthy as well. It's known as an Oxpecker, (or "tickbird"). About the size of a Starling they perch on animal's backs and eat disease carrying ticks and insects. And when danger stalks the grasslands the wary birds voice an alarm which alerts the animals to the danger.

Most animals seem to gladly tolerate the intrusion. The tickbirds even enter the wide-open mouth of sleeping crocodiles eating decayed flesh from between its teeth. (Who needs a dentist?!)

Because they do good and also warn of impending danger, I refer to them as "missionary birds." After all, Christian missionaries dedicate their lives to do good and to warn. Throughout this world missionaries have been responsible for setting up hospitals, schools, colleges, and churches. They also tell people of their need for salvation, and warn them of the disaster that falls upon people who do not accept this eternal gift from God.

Missionaries heed God's command in Ezekiel 33:7-9 (New Living Translation). "Now, son of man, I am making you a watchman for the people... [so] listen to what I say and warn them for me. If I announce that some wicked people are sure to die and you fail to warn them about changing their ways, then they will die in their sins, but I will hold you responsible for their deaths. But if you warn them to repent and they don't repent, they will die in their sins, but you will not be held responsible."

Yes, God wants every Christian to be a missionary. He wants them to warn the unsaved people of their impending eternal death, and tell them of God's rescue plan found in John 3:16, "...but God so loved the world that He gave His only Son, so that everyone who believes in Him will not perish but have eternal life."

The River Devil

The Piranha fish, also known as the "River Devil" swims in the vast basin of the Amazon River. No other fresh-water creature has such a grim reputation for aggressiveness and ferocity. Only about the size of a Sunfish, the Piranha killing machine involves swimming in schools of dozens to hundreds stalking the Amazon River in search of prey to satisfy their voracious appetites. When they find a victim, they attack it at full speed using their razor sharp, triangular teeth, to strip the flesh from it's bones, churning the water to foam and dying it red with blood.

As a result, Piranha infested waters present a unique problem for the Brazilian herdsmen as they free-graze their precious cattle from one grazing area to another. The reason is, from time to time, they have to herd them across the Amazon or one of its tributaries which harbors these killer fish.

The solution is both painful and expensive. In order to get the herd across to a better pasture, a cow has to be sacrificed by taking it downstream and forcing it into the river. Immediately the sacrificial beast is swarmed by the deadly Piranha, their jaws ripping the flesh with lightening speed. While the Piranha are feeding and distracted, the herdsmen quickly drive the rest of the cattle across in safety. In 20 minutes nothing is left of the sacrificial animal except a skeleton. But by this time the herd is safe on the other side.

NATURE-ly SPEAKING — a spiritual principle can be observed. Like the herd of cattle, mankind is in a similar predicament. He is stuck in a bad

The Bible says, "God is on one side and all the people on the other side, and Christ Jesus, Himself man, is between them to bring them together."

"pasture" (this earth) doomed for eternal death. However, there is another "pasture" (heaven) which guarantees eternal life. But the two pastures are separated by a "river" known as sin. Throughout history mankind has tried to get over that river of sin to salvation by bridging it with "good works," "church membership," and among a multitude of methods, "religions of many kinds." All totally useless. But, like the Brazilian herdsmen, God presented a solution to get His chosen "herd" across the sin-cursed gap. He provided His one and only Son to be a sacrifice, thus bridging the gap from eternal death to eternal life in Heaven. God allowed His Son, Jesus, to die a horrible death on a cross and then raised Him from the grave 3 days later. When Jesus died on the cross and rose from the grave, he paid the penalty for our sin and made it possible for mankind to attain heaven and eternal life rather than hell and eternal damnation.

The Bible says, "God is on one side and all the people on the other side, and Christ Jesus, Himself man, is between them to bring them together." (1 Timothy 2:5, Living Bible). To take advantage of God's sacrifice and ensure eternal life in Heaven, man must respond by believing that Jesus is the Christ, the Son of the Living God, and receive Him by personal acceptance. "But as many as receive Him, to them gave He power to become the sons of God, even to them that believe on His name. (John 1:12).

To do this simply pray and tell God you want to follow Him through faith in His Son, Jesus the Christ. Here's a sample prayer: Father in Heaven, I come to you in the name of your Son, Jesus Christ. I desire to be one of your children. I believe that Jesus Christ is the Son of God, that He died on the cross, was buried, and rose again, three days later. I believe this sacrifice was designed so that my sins will be washed away through his shed blood. I now accept Jesus Christ as my Personal Savior. Amen."

John 3:16 says, "For God so loved (put your name here), that He gave His only begotten Son, that if (put your name here) believes in Him, (put your name here) shall not perish, but (put your name here) will have everlasting life.

The Lion's Teeth

The creatures of the wild often depend on the power of their teeth for survival. A hungry lion will scan Africa's grassland for a suitable animal to kill. It is usually a zebra, wildebeest, or buffalo. When he spots his prey, the lion slinks toward the doomed beast taking every precaution to assure the attack will be a surprise. Using the tall sun-burnt grass as a camouflage he approaches to within a few feet of the unsuspecting prey. Then, with a swift pounce, the lion sinks his teeth into the animal's neck.

As the teeth of death sink deeply toward the jugular vein, the lion suddenly shifts his weight of 500 pounds and the animal flips to the ground with a neck-breaking jolt. But the lion keeps his teeth deeply embedded into the neck of his prey until all signs of life are gone. Then, it's time to eat.

NATURE-ly SPEAKING – a spiritual principle can be learned from the lion and his killer teeth. The Bible, in II Peter 5:8 typifies our enemy, Satan, as a "...lion seeking whom he may devour." The fact that there are so many "devoured" (or, backslidden) people living in a state of misery and defeat is a clear indication that Satan's tactics are very effective.

But there's a weapon against Satan's "lion" teeth. King David discovered it. He was so happy with the revelation he penned these words found in Psalm 124:6 (NLT): "Blessed be the Lord, who did not let their teeth tear us apart!" The secret weapon against lion's teeth (or, spiritual failure) is summed up in Nehemiah 9:28 (New Living Translation). Nehemiah is praying to God, telling him that His people were killing prophets, they were being disobedient, rebellious, and committing all kinds of blasphemies, yet when they got into trouble and called in repentance, God graciously forgave and helped them. But then after their time of repentance it seemed the cycle returned, yet, (verse 28), "...when all was going well, your people turned to sin again, and once more you let their enemies conquer them. Yet whenever your people cried to you again for help, you listened once more from heaven. In your wonderful mercy, you rescued them repeatedly!"

Yes, God is in the business of forgiving. He did it for them, he'll do it for us. Over and over again....

NATURE*ly*
SPEAKING

The Frozen Frog

O nce, before Photoshop computer software which enables graphic designers to do all kinds of fancy things to pictures, I had the task of producing a photographic image to illustrate an article about "double-mindedness." I had to do it the old-fashioned way. The plan was to take a double-exposure picture of a frog so it looked like one animal with two heads. The idea was simple. First, I'd take a picture of the frog looking one way, then I'd turn it around and take another picture of it facing the other way, all on the same piece of film. I set up a backdrop stage on my African porch, caught a frog in a nearby swamp, and went to work! Ha! Did you ever try to get a frog to sit still?

The first part of the picture was fairly simple. But turning it around for the double-exposure was the thing of which nightmares are made. The critter just would not sit still, even for a fraction of a second! Frustrated almost to tears, I tried to think of ways to get it to sit still. Evil thoughts of smearing glue on its underside to simply nailing the thing to a board crossed my mind, but were quickly dismissed as a bit "over the top." I needed a more humane way. A-hah! I remembered in my high school days a certain biology lesson told about hibernation. Frogs hibernate. Maybe, I reasoned, if I could get the frog to start a hibernation, he'd be less likely to jump around. But that presented the challenge of getting its body temperature to drop.

No problem. Over my wife's objections, I stuck the frog in the freezer. I promised her I'd take it out in about ten minutes. But no sooner did I place the frog in the freezer than some dear fellow missionaries came for a visit. By the time they left, it was dark and time to get the kids ready for bed. Everyone forgot about the frog. That is until the next morning when we were eating breakfast. Someone said, "The frog!" We all screamed, "The frog!" I rushed to the freezer not knowing what I'd find. I slowly and fearfully opened the freezer door. There he was, eyes wide open, a beautifully preserved solid chunk of frozen flesh! Fatefully I said, "I think its dead, but its preserved beautifully. Perfect for my picture." That was not, I repeat, not, the best choice of words. Of course my wife burst into tears while my children simply gave me that, "Dad, how could you...." look.

With a heavy heart, but still determined to get my picture, I took the frozen frog outside and took all kinds of pictures. No jumping around this time. My double-exposures went flawlessly. I worked fast because I was sure once it thawed I'd have a very dead frog on my hands, and I just wasn't in the mood to photograph a dead limp frog.

But then a remarkable thing happened. My son, Philip, saw it first. "Dad," he yelled, "the frog's eyes are moving!" Sure enough. Then there was a slow blink. Next its head moved ever so slightly. In short order the Kenya sun had that little fellow all thawed and hopping merrily around. My wife wiped her tears. My kids smiled again. Together we triumphantly carried him to the swamp. The last thing we ever saw of that little guy was when he took a giant leap and disappeared into his own special world of tall grass. (And, I'm sure, with quite a tale to tell....)

"Why," you might ask, "would a sane human being want to illustrate something like a "double-minded man?" Simple. Because the Bible says that God doesn't like or want His people to be that way.

Take, for example, Lot found in the Old Testament. He was a double-minded man who wanted to have it both ways — that is, to worship the true God of his uncle, Abraham, AND he wanted to enjoy the pleasures of this world which the evil city of Sodom provided. Actually he moved his family into the city and even sat proudly at Sodom's gate as one of it's elders. He was a straddler. Neither hot nor cold. So compromised was he that when he tried to tell his married daughters and their husbands that they should flee Sodom because God was going to destroy it, they wouldn't believe him nor would anyone else.

Not only that, but when judgment fell, only his wife and two daughters still living at home escaped. And even during the escape, his wife was so attached to the city she disobeyed by looking back. She died instantly. (Read the story for yourself in Genesis 19.) What tragedy "double-mindedness" brought to this family.

It seems God interprets "double-mindedness" as a blending of the spiritual with the worldly. Or, as the book of Revelation says, someone who is neither hot nor cold, but lukewarm. Actually, the Holy Spirit inspired the writer of the book of James to use "double-mindedness" as the overall theme of the book.

While we are not saved by our good deeds, they certainly mirror our faith. As an example James 2:14-18 teaches, "What good is it, my brothers, if a man claims to have faith but has no deeds? Can such faith save him? Suppose a brother or sister is without clothes and daily food. 'Go, I wish you well; keep warm and well fed,' but does nothing about his physical needs, what good is it? In the same way, faith by itself, if it is not accompanied by action, is dead. But someone will say, 'You have faith; I have deeds.' Show me your faith without deeds, and I will show you my faith by what I do."

The Case of the Long-eared Look-alikes

When is a rabbit a hare? Never.

Even though they look alike, the rabbit and the hare are distinctly two different animals. Yet they are often mistaken for each other.

For example, the Belgian Hare is not a hare, but a rabbit. The Jack Rabbit is not a rabbit, but a hare.

The World Book Encyclopedia gives a simple identity test: "The animals can be told apart most easily at birth. A newborn rabbit is blind, it has no fur, and cannot move about. Whereas a newborn hare can see, it has a coat of fine fur, and it can hop a few hours after birth."

NATURE-ly SPEAKING a Spiritual lesson can be learned from the long-eared look-alikes.

Even as there are deceptive "look-alikes" in the animal kingdom, so there are deceptive "look-alikes" in Christendom.

The Bible clearly warns of "look-alikes" in the form of false Christs, teachers and leaders. Matthew 24:24 says, "false messiahs and false prophets will rise up and perform great miraculous signs and wonders so as to deceive, if possible, even God's chosen ones."

How can we tell the difference?

Even as there is an identity test to tell the difference between a rabbit and a hare, so there is a simple identity test to expose the dishonest "Christian" leaders.

First, check their "birth." Were they redeemed by Jesus' sacrifice on the cross, and do they believe in His resurrection from the dead?

The Bible says, "Many deceivers have gone into the world. They do not believe that Jesus Christ came to earth in a real body. Such a person is a deceiver and an antichrist. Watch out, so that you do not lose the prize for which we have been working so hard. Be diligent so that you will receive your full reward. For if you wander beyond the teaching of Christ, you will not have fellowship with God. But if you continue in the teaching of Christ, you will have fellowship with both the Father and the Son. If someone comes to your meeting and does not teach the truth about Christ, don't invite him into your house or encourage him in any way. Anyone who encourages him becomes a partner in his evil work. (2 John 7-10, New Living Translation Bible.)

What did Christ teach? (Here's a list of some of His teachings and the Bible passages where these teachings can be found. Any version of the Bible is fine, however, I prefer the New Living Translation Bible.)

Salvation (John chapter 3.)
End of the World (Matthew, chapters 24 and 25.)
Life after death (Luke 18:28-30.)
Sex (Matthew 5:28,29.)
Christian living (Matthew, Chapters 5, 6, & 7.)

Carefully study the teachings of Jesus and you'll never have to worry about "look-alikes."

NATURE*ly* SPEAKING

Eagle Wisdom

For fifteen years my family and I lived on the edge of Kenya's Great Rift Valley on a mission station known as Kijabe. It's 7500 feet above sea level. Below on the valley floor, when the sun is shining on African villages and herds of domestic and wild animals, Kijabe is often "fogged in" by clouds.

But one nice thing about living in the clouds is that Eagles also like to hang out at this altitude. Actually about two miles from my home a pair of Eagles lived along the jagged cliffs. The nest was snuggled rather precariously on an overhanging ledge, sheltered from the elements by jutting rocks. Since Eagles use their nests year after year it becomes bulky and heavy as they repair and add to it season after season. Some reports say a nest can weigh as much as a ton! It's built with sticks of all sizes.

To see this nest I had to climb down, rather than up, the cliff. I didn't want to disturb them, so using binoculars I observed them from a respectable distance. I even noticed some bones woven into the nest. Once the large basic infrastructure was built to accommodate about five large birds the holes and gaps were filled with smaller sticks from thorn bushes and other jaggy stuff. This was then covered with lots and lots of soft items such as skins of animals, leaves, rags, and, I swear some of my long lost t-shirts. The thorns and jaggy stuff kept it from blowing away. Pretty smart.

On the ledge, next to the huge nest, was a flat slab, which was used as a

As I looked down and saw all the dark swirling clouds below I also noticed something else, an eagle flying, not through the storm, but above it.

runway for a fast take-off. I read that Eagle pairs live together beside the nest and are devoted to one another. This was certainly true of the pair I was watching.

Usually the female lays one to three eggs, which start hatching in about 35 days. Their care for the young is very interesting. When the young eaglets are old enough to fly (about 10 – 13 weeks after hatching) the parents disrupt the comfortable nest by "stirring" it up! That is, they attack it (almost like a housecleaning) by tossing out the soft skins, rags, and leaves. Rather than having a place of peaceful rest as before, the eaglets are now confronted with a nest that pokes and jags and hurts. The ploy works and the eaglets leave their comfort zone and walk on the ledge runway. Daily they start flapping their wings, building flight muscle. Through some instinct, along with a parent's urging the young birds try their wings in flight. If, as the little one flies downward and the parent notices it is having difficulty, the parent swoops down swiftly and spreads its wings under the little one catching it from a fatal fall. I'm sure this is what the Bible means in Deut. 32:11, "As an eagle stirreth up her nest, fluttereth over her young, spreadeth abroad her wings, taketh them, beareth them on her wings."

NATURE-ly SPEAKING – several spiritual lessons can be learned from the Eagle. Sometimes, when God wants to move us, He makes our "nest" uncomfortable so that we are forced from our comfort zone into an exciting unknown. But as we go he promises to never put more on us than we are able to bear. He promises in Exodus 19:4, "You know how I brought you to myself and carried you on eagle's wings." He reminded them of their wilderness journey and of the times their food and water supply dwindled, but He never failed them. At the right moment, He reminded them, He "carried them on eagle's wings." His care for us, His children, is like the mother eagle's care for her young. With God on our side we can afford to take risks.

Eagles fly above storms. One day I was in an AIM/AIR plane heading to an assignment when the pilot saw a storm brewing ahead of us. No problem, he simply nosed the airplane up over the storm, away from the turbulence. As I looked down and saw all the dark swirling clouds below I also noticed something else, an eagle flying, not through the storm, but above it. When life comes at us with all its billowing thunder and wind, when catastrophe is all around, when things seem to be hopeless, as it was for David in the story found in 1 Samuel 30:1- 25 (please read), what did he do? vs. 4 says, "But David found strength in the Lord his God." He went above the storm for victory.

Eagles have other birds who often fly after them trying to steal away a fish or rodent catch they just made. How does the eagle deal with this enemy? When such an attack occurs he will immediately put himself between the aggressor and the sun. By flying directly into the rays of the sun, the enemy quickly loses sight of him and simply gives up. Likewise, as we get nearer to God the "Son," Satan and other evil forces cannot touch us. "Those who live in the shelter of the Most High will find rest in the shadow of the Almighty. (Psalm 91:1).

Elephants on the Road

My friend, Hal Olsen, is a creative missionary journalist. While living in Kenya he was often amused by roadside signs which read "Attention: Elephants have the right away!" After all any motorist who suddenly comes face to face with a couple tons of elephant doesn't need a sign to tell him the evident facts of life. So, one day he sat down at his typewriter (yes, that's what was used in those days) and wrote a story about the signs for several magazines. That was many, many moons ago, and I lost or misplaced his original story, but I wanted to include it in this book, so, with Hal's blessing I've written a facsimile. Here's my rendition of Hal's story.

"Road signs along African roads read, 'Attention: Elephants have the right of way.' Of course, any motorist who suddenly comes face to face with a couple tons of elephant, doesn't need a sign to tell him the evident facts of life.

"The tragedy is that often a nighttime driver, enthralled by the sight, will flash on high-beam lights to get a better look. This, of course, disturbs the elephant and hours later the driver might very well arrive at his destination in a car that looks like he took a joy ride through a war zone.

"A wise nighttime driver will do several things when he encounters an elephant. First, he'll stop slowly and then turn off the motor. Next, he'll either dim his lights or turn them off completely. This way the elephant will see the silent, dark vehicle simply as an obstacle and will go around it. No damage done."

NATURE-ly SPEAKING — a spiritual lesson can be learned from this simple, common sense proceedure. Spiritually, light causes opposition from the Satanic enemy. Dim you light, or better still, turn it off completely, and, like the elephant, your satanic enemy will not become agitated and will disappear. After all, Jesus said correctly, "...men love darkness rather than light...." (That goes for Satan and his demons too.) And yes, Jesus was crucified because the powers of darkness couldn't stand the awful exposure the light of His teachings brought. Even today, Christians who faithfully witness to the light found in Christ are open to demonic attacks by Satan and his cohorts.

Therefore...Christians have a decision to make! Dim or douse the light and be free from enemy attack! Or, obey the command of Christ found in Matthew 5:15, 16, "Don't hide your light...instead put it on a stand and let it shine for all. In the same way, let your good deeds shine out for all to see...."

So, my fellow Christians, when we're surrounded by spiritual "Elephants" it seems the Bible wants us to let our lights shine brightly even if we have to take (gulp!) a few lumps for Jesus. After all, because of His lumps we have Salvation and Eternal life!

P.S. — However, if you ever travel on an African road, watch out for real elephants and follow these instructions v-e-r-y c-a-r-e-f-u-l-l-y.

NATURE*ly* SPEAKING

The World's Meanest Mother

The female ostrich has the unenviable reputation as being one of the worst mothers in the animal kingdom. It seems she has no "mothering" instincts whatsoever. Immediately after laying her eggs she wanders off looking after no one but herself, leaving the male to take over the job of incubating them during the 8 week process. She has no concern for the male who sits under the burning African sun, growing thinner day by day. Even after the eggs hatch she takes no responsibility in caring for the young. It's the male who looks after the young and teaches them to fend for themselves.

NATURE-ly SPEAKING — there is a spiritual lesson to be learned. The Bible clearly teaches that the father is the HEAD of the home, but the mother is the HEART of the home. Someone has said, "A nation is as strong as the character of our mothers."

I recall reading a short article entitled, "The Meanest Mother." I have no idea who wrote it, but I clipped it out of the paper and put it in my file to be used "sometime." That "sometime" is now.

The unknown author wrote, "I had the meanest mother in the world. While other kids ate candy for breakfast, I had to eat cereal, eggs and toast. When others had coke and candy for lunch, I had to eat a sandwich. As you can guess, my dinner was different from other kids.

"My mother insisted on knowing where I was at all times. She had to know who my friends were and what we were doing. She insisted that if I told her I would be gone an hour, I would be gone for an hour or less.

"I'm ashamed to admit it, but she actually had the nerve to make us kids work. We had to wash dishes, make beds, and learn to cook. I believe she stayed awake at night, thinking up things for me to do!

"By the time I became a teenager, she had grown even meaner. She embarrassed me by making my dates come to the front door and pick me up. And while my friends were dating at the mature age of 12 and 13, my old-fashioned mother refused to let me date until I was 16.

"In spite of the harsh way I was raised, I've never been arrested. And all my brothers and sisters turned out okay, too. I guess we owe it all to our mean mother. She insisted that we grow up into God-fearing, honest, responsible adults.

"I'm grateful to God that he gave me the meanest mother in the world!"

Moths that Drink Elephant Tears

Yes, there are moths that drink the tears of elephants! Known as Mabra elephantophila this particular species of moth is shy, tiny, and delicate. It's remarkable behavior astonished entomologists when first discovered. Scientists now believe that, because tears contain not only salt and water but also trace levels of protein, they become a very nutritious source of food for moths. And, the Mabra elephantophila, because of its tiny size is able to feast on tears without the elephant even noticing.

But hold on, there are other moths that feast on tears as well. Most, it seems, prefer the tears of large hoofed mammals such as the wet eyes of horses, deer, tapirs, pigs, and occasionally, people. For some reason, they shy away from tears of carnivores such as dogs and cats.

It seems each species of moth has its own unique technique for extracting tears. For example, there is one moth that lands silently beside the eye of the victim. Then, very carefully, it sweeps its proboscis (the long slender tubular feeding and sucking "nose" structure) across the eye of its host, irritating the eyeball, which then produces tears. Another species waits until the animal is asleep at which time it is able to insert it's proboscis under the eyelid and drink away! But the poor moth, Poncetia, has such a short proboscis it must cling to the eyeball itself to drink. For this moth timing is of utmost importance, because if the weeping host blinks, more often than not dear ol' Poncetia will never drink, or for that matter, fly again. Imagine the ignominy of being crushed to death by, of all things, an eyelid!

NATURE-ly SPEAKING — even as moths gain life-giving sustenance from animal tears, likewise we can spiritually feed ourselves with Biblical "tears." Four of my favorite Biblical "tear" stories are as follows:

The tears of a Queen. (Read the entire book of Esther, preferably from the New Living Translation, it's a fast read!) The story of Queen Esther is a thrilling story of God placing the right person at the right place at the right time to save His people. I never tire of reading this story over and over again. In journalistic lingo, it falls into the category of the "biter gets bit." In other words the bad guy gets his payback. The tears in this story don't start flowing until the 8th chapter. But when the beautiful queen presented her petition to the king with flowing tears, he was moved and the process of redemption was put into action. The tears revealed Esther's earnestness, her devotion, and her purpose of heart. Praying with tears is very effective. Oh, that we would shed tears while upon our knees.

The tears of a King: (2 Kings 20:5 and 6). Poor King Hezekiah received word from the prophet that he was going to die. Through the prophet, God said to the King, "Set your affairs in order for you are going to die. You will not recover from this illness." When Hezekiah heard this he broke down and wept saying, "Remember, O Lord, how I have always tried to be faithful to you and do what is pleasing in your sight." Then God said, "I have heard your prayer and seen your tears. I will heal you...." In this case a simple prayer mixed with tears brought another 15 years of life to King Hezekiah.

The tears of a sinner: (Luke 7:36-50). This story tells of a sinful woman so repentant that she shed bitter tears, which fell upon the feet of her Savior, Jesus the Christ. She then wiped them off with her hair. Jesus saw those tears, which revealed her true repentance. He in return gave her the eternal salvation she so desperately desired. Oh, would more people fall at Jesus' feet with true repentance and tears.

The tears of a missionary: (Psalm 126:5,6). The key words in this passage are: "They that sow in tears shall reap in joy." A missionary is one who anguishes over the fate of people without Christ. The tears flow because missionaries are aware of the eternal tragedy that awaits anyone who has not yet received the good seed into his heart. The joy comes when the lost sheep and the lost coin (as explained in Luke 15) are found. Yes, joy, when a lost sinner is found and redeemed with eternal life by believing on the Lord Jesus Christ. "For God so loved the world that he gave his only begotten son that whosoever believes in Him, should not perish, but have everlasting life." John 3:16.

Praying with tears usually indicates a heart made malleable by a deep faith and a broken, humble spirit. Dry-eyed prayers can sometimes come from dry hearts. And dry hearts do not always produce the heavenly flowers that bloom from ones fed by nutritious tears.

NOTES

NOTES

NOTES